Coaching Coaches

… for players, parents, and coaches from youth through high school age sports

By Coach Finnie

To order additional copies of this title, contact your local bookstore or go to www.coachingcoaches.net.

Printed and bound in the United States of America

Coach Finnie is proud of coaching players in different sports in the ages of 5-18 and working with their parents on recreational, select, and off-season high school teams.

Table of Contents

Pre-Game

Coaches of youth through high school age sports come in all sizes, shapes, and colors. They are of different ages, ethnicity, and socio-economic backgrounds. But coaches do not come trained.

Coaches may know how to kick, run, shoot, and throw. Coaches may know about batting averages, free throw shooting, and football punting hang time. But do they understand how to work with, communicate with, and relate to people of various ages?

Little people that are ages 5-9.

A little bigger people that are ages 10-14.

Or high school people, ages 15-18.

And include the moms and dads of those people.

That is the purpose of this book. Improving the sports life for all of those involved by opening the lines of communication between the three key groups in sports for ages 5-18: players, parents and coaches!

"I like the dreams of the future better than the history of the past." Thomas Jefferson

This book is based on three important experiences of the author:

1. observing sports for more than 50 years.

2. playing sports for more than 40 years.

3. coaching sports for more than 30 years.

It's said that a tourist once spotted Pablo Picasso sketching in a Paris café and asked if he would sketch her, offering to pay him fair value. In a matter of minutes, Picasso was finished. When she asked what she owed him, Picasso told her 5,000 francs.

"But it only took you a few minutes," the tourist said.

"No," said Picasso, "it took me all my life." from the Wall Street Journal

It does not matter what the sport is. Just because you played it or watched it does not mean you can coach it.

It does not matter who the player is. Just because you are the parent does not mean you can coach your child.

You may have been the best athlete or the least skilled athlete.

You may have been the best student or the one who struggled with the books.

You may be a wonderful parent or the one who just wonders about parenting.

You may be a great businessperson or the one who has no business being in business.

You may be a teacher of the year in the classroom or the one who knows no subject.

It does not mean you can automatically coach a child in grammar school, a middle school youth, or a high school age young man or woman. You need assistance, or more importantly, to first become an assistant to an experienced, knowledgeable and relevant coach.

If you are a volunteer coach, you should be applauded for your noble effort and precious time commitment. Volunteer coaches are critical to sports being played throughout these age groups. But even a volunteer needs to know what to do.

If you are a paid coach, you should be applauded for the extra effort and the extra time put in. Paid coaches are important, especially in the high school years. But even a paid coach must know what to do.

This book is meant for parents in what to look for and what to expect with the numerous coaches in various sports you come across now and in the years ahead. Parenting is a huge commitment for the first 18 years of a child's life and dealing with coaches in the sports your child participates in can add to the enjoyment or the difficulty of the sports life. It should be enjoyable.

"The half of knowledge is knowing where to find it."
Samuel Johnson

There is an old coaching joke on the two best places to coach:

1. An orphanage because no parents are involved.

2. A prison because no alumni are involved.

But it does not have to be this way. Too many coaches have created a monarchy, with a king coach or a queen coach settled in for the balance of history. Make proclamations and only communicate with a posting on a door. That is why this book is also for the new coach or the veteran coach.

"To lead the people, walk behind them." Lao-Tze

The new coach can get a jump-start. It is far too often where a young adult starts immediately as a head coach of an off-season team (e.g., coaching a basketball team during the summer months), or a select team or even as the freshmen or junior varsity coach in high school without any coaching experience.

Is that fair to the players? Is that fair to the parents? Is that fair to the coach?

Internships, apprenticeships, and student teaching work in many occupations. Why not with coaching in the 5-18 age group? Assisting an experienced, knowledgeable and relevant coach for a minimum of two years in a sport should be a requirement before taking over the responsibility of leading any youth to high school age group in that sport. And just because you coached in one sport doesn't mean you know how to coach another sport.

"Good enough seldom is." Malcolm Forbes

And this book is also for the experienced coach. But only one who is willing to be challenged in his or her thinking. To paraphrase Jeffrey Gitomer, a consultant to many business executives and sales organizations, is he or she a coach of many different years, or the same year 15, 20, or 25 times over?

"Stay new." Jeffrey Gitomer

Finally, this book is for the young people of today and tomorrow. Very few athletes will be professionals in a sport they participate in. But that is not why you should participate in any sport. Sports are a great way to make friends, to learn new things, and to stay out of trouble.

Also, young people from ages 5-18 need to look at the sports they enjoy as lifelong sports. Not just bowling, golf, running, softball, or swimming. Any sport.

Yes, any sport is a life-long thrill. Be active, stay in shape, and you can do baseball, basketball, skiing, soccer, and any other sport you want to throw in here. You can play the sport for a lifetime.

Everyone owes it to the young people of today and tomorrow to keep them excited about their sports. Sports provide an unbelievable outlet for energy and time. A coach at any level, ages 5-9, ages 10-14, or ages 15-18, can have a major impact on whether a player stays with a sport up to and throughout high school and many years beyond.

"The future depends on what we do in the present."
Mahatma Gandhi

The coaching model needs to change. The doors of communication need to open wide. Open wide to a three way street to accommodate the player, the parents, and the coach. All of these people involved need to know and understand their role in the development of an athlete in sports and a person in life at each level.

A player can then accept the reality of the athletic life. Parents can then accept the reality of their child's life and a coach can then accept the results of their efforts without concern over player disappointment and parent second-guessing.

"Man cannot discover new oceans unless he has the courage to lose sight of the shore." Author Unknown

Coaches will make mistakes since they are human. Coaches will be second-guessed since it is natural for others to think they know better even before sports talk radio existed. But too many coaches rely on the X's and O's of their sport, the technical aspects of how a sport is played. The people to people skills of a coach will have the biggest effect on players and parents, not the immediate outcome of a game or a season.

Many coaches, from the youngest age levels to the varsity level in high school, rely on the trite phrase "I'm in it for the kids." Now let's hold them to it.

After all, there is a reason coach is the best five letter word you can be called.

"Most of the important things in the world have been accomplished by people who have kept on trying when there seemed to be no hope at all." Dale Carnegie

First Period

Warm Ups

A 3-year-old boy (Boy 1) and his 5-year-old brother (Boy 2) were playing baseball with their Dad at the local schoolyard. Boy 1 was pitching to Dad and Boy 2 was playing in short left field. Dad hit a pitch over the head of Boy 2 in the outfield. As Dad was jogging to first base, he figured he would be near third base by the time Boy 2 threw the ball back to the infield. Dad yelled to Boy 1 standing on the pitching mound to "cover third base." Boy 1 went over to third base, Boy 2 was retrieving the hit ball, and Dad was then nearing second base. As Dad approached third base, the throw from Boy 2 was rolling in to the infield and Boy 1 was on the ground pushing dirt on top of third base. Dad asked Boy 1 "what are you doing?" Boy 1 (the 3 year old) responded to his Dad "You told me to cover third base!"

Ages 5-9

This is five years of joy in youth sports. Sport is pure recreation. It is fun and games all the time, even in organized events. At least it should be.

TIME OUT: THESE FIVE YEARS ARE FOR RECREATIONAL SPORTS. THERE SHOULD NOT BE ANY SELECT, CLUB, OR TRAVEL LEVEL TEAMS IN THIS AGE GROUP. FOCUS ON FUN AND FUNDAMENTALS. (We talk more about these special types of teams in the next age group.)

The player thinks he or she is a little star. Team shirts or uniforms are provided. Equipment for the sport is used. Individual and team pictures are taken. Everything is like the big leagues in the eyes of the child.

The parent believes the player is a little star. The sign up date is met. The schedules are put on the refrigerator. The player's equipment is purchased. Individual and team pictures are bought. Every athletic step taken is important in the mind of the parent.

"You don't know what the future holds, but you know who holds the future." Author Unknown

TIME OUT: THE PARENTS REALLY HELP THE COACH OUT AT THIS AGE LEVEL IF THEY INFORM THE COACH AT THE START OF THE SEASON THEY HAVE A SPECIAL NEEDS PLAYER INVOLVED IN THE SPORT. AT THIS AGE GROUP IT IS EASY TO HAVE A SPECIAL NEEDS PLAYER MIXED IN WITH THE OTHER PLAYERS BECAUSE OF THE EMPHASIS ON RECREATION. BUT TELL THE COACH. DON'T LEAVE IT UP TO HIM OR HER TO FIGURE IT OUT AFTER ONE OR TWO PRACTICES.

The coach is usually a volunteer for the sports in this age group. Intentions are usually good, but the experience and knowledge of the person in the sport can be limited. He or she may have played the sport. He or she may be a parent. But the coach needs to feel like a player <u>and</u> a parent during this time.

In most sports the object is for players to score points of some kind. A coach can also score points with players and parents if the coach makes the time spent with the sport interesting, enjoyable and timely for all involved.

Here is a three pointer scored for the coach if he or she feels how it is to be a player:

1. Who is stuck in right field every game

2. Who is the last player in the game every time

3. Who never gets the ball in any part of the game

And here is a three pointer scored for the coach if he or she feels how it is to be a parent:

1. Who is waiting for their son or daughter to get into the game

2. Who is waiting for practice to get over after the planned completion time

3. Who is watching their son or daughter make mistakes every game

In this age group, most sport leagues have playing time requirements. But these are minimum requirements. Coaches need to go <u>beyond</u> the minimums. If the minimums are 15 minutes in a 40-minute basketball game, it does not mean the lesser skilled players only get 15 minutes for each game and the better skilled get more. It does mean each player gets the chance for the extra minutes over the course of the season. The number of games played and the variety of skill levels of the other teams in a league makes it easy to vary the quantity of playing time for all players, not just the best ones.

Also, coaches need to vary the starting lineups, giving each player a chance to start. Even at this age there is a thrill to be in at the beginning of the game.

Finally, coaches need to vary the positions, giving each player a chance to play different positions. Even special positions like baseball catcher or soccer goalkeeper need to be part of the player rotation. Regardless of the sport, there are enough positions for everyone to learn and to enjoy.

SPORT SAMPLE: **The big player at 9 years old can play the guard position in basketball as well as the center position in a game. The skills learned at a young age can be transferred between positions. After all, how do you know the player will be big forever?**

Coaches will give excuses for not doing these things, but no excuses are warranted. You can work around the different skill levels at these ages. Players do not need to be stuck in a single role at such an early age in their sport life.

SPORT SAMPLE: **In t-ball or even coached pitched youth baseball, the players with a higher skill level can play first base, shortstop and the pitching mound. At this age the players will usually hit the ball to the middle of the field and you need a player with a higher skill at first base to catch throws. That leaves six other field positions for players to be placed in and rotated around if they do not have the higher skills yet. This player strategy benefits everyone. The defense won't be bored in the field if three outs can be achieved sooner than if the opposing team is batting through their lineup each inning. And then the defensive team**

leaves the positions in the field and becomes the offense to get the chance to hit again!

One of the greatest thrills for a coach is to see a player progress. When a player with limited interest and limited skills can stay involved in a youth sports program, a thrill can happen. The catch of a pop fly by such a 9-year-old player, even if it is by sticking the glove in the air and hoping, is unforgettable.

"The saddest kind of failure is when you aim low and miss." Brandon Tartikoff

Coaching this age group is a great way to learn coaching, the same way it is a great way to learn officiating. Local sports groups are anxious to train teenage youth to officiate in this age group. What about a teenage youth being an assistant coach in this age group? This is a perfect time for teens to learn coaching before being involved with older age groups. Even on a part time basis. The pool of coaching candidates needs to go beyond the parents of the players.

Some parents begin coaching their own child at this time. Coaching your own child is not easy at these ages or any ages. A coach will know more about their own child's skills and that is good and bad. It is good because the more you know the more you can help that child. But a parent needs to avoid favoritism at these early ages so the child doesn't expect that type of treatment at a later stage in their athletic career when the parent may not be as involved with their athletic development.

Also, the coaching parent needs to avoid being harder and more demanding on their own child than on his or her teammates. It is important to separate the coaching role from the parent role with the son or daughter. A coach needs to avoid the challenge of expecting more of his or her own child than what is reasonable. Being tougher on your own son or daughter is no better than being easier on them. A "whipping boy or girl" is unnecessary for any age, especially for your own child.

"Nothing else can quite substitute for a few well-chosen, well-timed, sincere words of praise. They're absolutely free, and worth a fortune." Sam Walton

This is a great time for the coaches, and even the officials, to provide game time instruction on fundamentals. Since the emphasis is on recreation, coaches can explain how to improve skill levels during the course of the game in addition to during practice time. Depending upon the age and the league rules, coaches can go on the playing surface to explain to a player how to best perform a particular skill. It is important to go to a player or have the player come to you when they are out of the game. There is no need to yell out and highlight a player's shortcomings.

This is also an excellent time for an official to point out to a player what they should change to prevent being called for a rule violation. Tell the coaches at the beginning of the game that you will stop play to quietly mention to the player what they need to change before you call the infraction. Be sure to tell the player's coach at the same time what the violation is so he or she can reinforce the change the player needs to make.

SPORT SAMPLE: **In youth basketball when a player has a tendency to carry the basketball instead of dribbling, then it is time for instruction to occur. The player will put his or her hand underneath the**

basketball to get the ball down the court instead of keeping the hand on top of the basketball. The official can help correct this by not calling the violation, but instead, stopping play and explaining to the player and the coach what needs to be done differently so the player does not gain an unfair advantage. The coach needs to appreciate this explanation from the official and reinforce it with the player.

Practice time for 5-9 year olds is a special time. Players think it is pretty cool to be getting together with other kids. Parents think they play a vital sports role in getting their child to a practice or involved in a car pool with other parents. And they do.

Here are nine points a coach of ages 5-9 <u>scores</u> when it comes to practice time:

1. Know the players first names by the second team event (practice or game) and call each player by first name. All the time.

2. Have the players introduce themselves to the team by saying their name and their school at the first few team events. The players will get to know each other and it is another way for the coaches to learn the names of the players.

3. Teach the fundamentals of the sport. How to hold the racket, the glove, etc. Remember many players in these ages are trying the sport to see if they may like it. Stick to the basics, but keep the basics interesting.

4. Involve additional parents. The more parents to help at a practice or a game, the better it will be.

Or invite a local high school or college athlete to help when available. The extra help will keep the players busy. Multiple practice drills take place at the same time. Instruct the parents on what you want done. With enough help the coach can supervise the drills and not just run them. (And the parents will learn it is not easy to coach and they will learn that their little star may not twinkle all the time.)

5. Make sure you talk to any parents who have older children playing sports in the middle school or high school age, but have a player in this age range as well. They will forget what a 5-9 year old needs to learn in this age range. Players will not be going home to "work" on their game. They will be going home to play tag with friends or the latest video game. And they should.

6. Plan out practices in your mind and on paper. Know what you want to do and when. At this age players should start to love practices, not detest them.

7. Expect the players to learn. Expect the parents to learn. Expect the coach to learn.

"When you're through improving, you're through." University of Michigan locker room sign

8. Keep it simple. Keep it short. Just 60 to 90 minutes for any practice for ages 5-9.

9. Keep everything on schedule.

> **TIME OUT**: YOU WILL WIN OVER EVERY PARENT IF YOU GIVE THEM A SCHEDULE OF DATES AND TIMES OF PRACTICES BEFORE THE SPORT SEASON BEGINS AND STICK TO IT.

10. BONUS POINT! There are no off-season practices or games. If they want to play the sport in the off-season, let them do it on their own in the driveway, at the park, or at the local athletic club. Playing with friends without adult supervision is good for any ages, even 5-9 year olds!

"One thing parents can't be is other children to their children." Author Unknown

If you are a coach in a sport, know the rules of the sport. If you are a coach in a league, know the rules of the league. If you don't know the rules, learn them. If you don't know and learn the rules, don't coach and don't comment. Just enjoy being a spectator.

SPORT SAMPLE: **Soccer is the classic example of a sport still unknown to many American parents. Oh, the parents think they know it and they think they can coach it. And they think they know it better than the officials. But it is more than running and kicking. Just ask any youth official!**

Coaches need to meet the officials before the game. In this age group, players need to see the importance officials have in a game. Players need to see the respect shown by coaches to officials. The players have not been involved in an organized sport before. They need to see there are rules to be followed and that officials will enforce the rules of the sport.

Also, usually the sports officials of ages 5-9 are teenagers or young adults who are just starting out in the officiating world. Don't discourage them. Don't argue with them. Officials are needed now and in the future. This is their training ground too. If the coach has a question, bring it up quietly with the official. Even better, bring it up quietly after the game is completed.

The behavior of the coach will influence the behavior of the players, parents and fans. The coach is a role model. Take it seriously. Take it proudly. Take it every practice and every game.

"What you do speaks so well. There's no need to hear what you say." Chuck Knox

Here are seven points to score for coaches of ages 5-9 at game time:

1. Meet the other team's coaches.

2. Meet the game officials.

3. Know your starting lineup before you are at the game.

4. Know when you plan to substitute even if subject to change.

5. Let the kids play – they won't remember the score of the game.

6. Behave – you are the role model for players and parents.

7. Thank officials after the game.

8. BONUS POINT! Be sure all players and coaches shake or touch hands in a friendly manner after the game.

SPORT SAMPLE: **In a city 3rd/4th grade league basketball championship game of 10 players on one team and 12 players on the other team, only one of the 22 players played high school varsity basketball for one of the two city high schools when those players reached the varsity age level. This is a typical example of why this age group needs to focus on the fun and fundamentals and not the win.**

In this age group it is up to the parents to make sure the coaches are doing the right things, noted above, for the players and the parents. The players are too young, and inexperienced in sports, to know what is happening to them. The parents need to make sure they talk with the coach if they have a question or a concern. The best way is to ask the coach for a few minutes after a practice or after a game and have that discussion in person and privately. But make sure you are cool and calm, and have allowed some time to pass before making the contact.

The second best way is to make the contact over the telephone. There is no third way.

And do it early in the season. If you are not successful after at least two attempts, then take your concern to the person running the league. But, also, have that discussion in person and privately. A telephone call can work too.

And don't talk about it with other players' parents. Give the coach a chance and, later, the league a chance, before you make a bigger deal out of it by involving other parents. A coach's intentions are usually good, but sometimes a coach gets caught up in the emotions of the moment and makes a poor decision. As a parent, you want to make sure a decision is best for your child and the team. Don't challenge a coach or a league just to show how smart you are.

"The happiest people don't necessarily have the best of everything; they just make the best of everything." Author Unknown

These steps are necessary to open that door of communication. The communication should be between the coach and player, the player and parent, and the coach and parent. It should not be between parents in the bleachers or on the sidelines. The coach and parents can prevent that sport cancer from happening at this early athletic age. Like any cancer, stop it early and the prognosis for a successful outcome improves.

"You gotta know happy, you gotta know glad because you're gonna know lonely and you're gonna know sad.

Sometimes you're the windshield, sometimes you're the bug.

Sometimes it all comes together, sometimes you're a fool in love.

Sometimes you're the Louisville slugger, sometimes you're the ball.

Sometimes it all comes together, sometimes you lose it all.

Everything can change in the blink of an eye so let the good times roll before we say goodbye." Mary-Chapin Carpenter from her song, The Bug

Second Inning

Warm Ups

A coach placed the telephone call to the player's house to inform him of the result of the 12-year-old select baseball team tryout. The player's mother answered the phone and said she could take the message, although the coach wanted to talk to the player. When the mother persisted, the coach told her the player did not make the team and why. The mother said she knew he did not have a chance from the start of the tryout.

The coach explained to her in the previous year there had been a turnover of three players out of a 14-player roster. An older son's team had turnovers of five players and four players the previous two years. The mother then realized the tryouts were legitimate and she had made incorrect assumptions based on how other area baseball teams had performed tryouts.

Guilty by association can happen to even good intentions in sports.

Ages 10-14

Fun is still here. Or it should be.

But the choices in sports and teams increase along with expectations.

There are more choices in the sports available and the team levels in the sports. Sports like football, hockey, volleyball, and wrestling become available to this age group. The primary sports of ages 5-9, sports like baseball, basketball, and soccer, expand from recreational teams to also include school, select, club, and travel teams. (Yes, there are some of these teams in the younger age group of 5-9, but they don't belong there as discussed earlier.)

Besides the expansion of choices in sports and teams, there are expectations. The expectations have expanded as well. Expectations of the player, the parent, and the coach have grown from the experiences of the younger ages and from what is viewed in the media.

"You live life looking forward, you understand life looking backward." Soren Kierkegard

Players have had a taste of sports and playing with and against others. They have watched the college and pro sports in person and through the media. They have expectations of when they will be on *SportsCenter*.

Parents have had a chance to drop off, pick up, and yell out. Little Johnny and Speedy Sue have become stars in waiting. The Sports *American Idol* is on their horizon.

Coaches have had to sweep off, line up, and set out. The teams to be coached are names like the Arsenal, Cubs, and Packers. Could this be the way Joe Torre, Pat Summit, and Bill Belichek started?

All of these visions of sports grandeur lead to the worst expectation of all for sports in this age group: winning.

Second Inning: Ages 10-14

Winning doesn't matter at this age group either, but the expectation of it affects what happens.

"Full effort equals full victory." Mahatma Gandhi

Additional opportunities arise for coaching in this age grouping. Besides recreational sports, there are select, club, and travel teams. Many similarities exist between select, club, and travel including tryouts, higher player fees, more practices, more games, and more time commitment. There is even year round time commitment in some cases.

The differences between select, club, and travel teams are usually the distance traveled for events and for player recruitment. Club and travel teams are willing to go far and wide in search of better competition and better players. Select teams may stay closer to home for most of their games and may have a geographic restriction on player eligibility.

Also, depending on the sport, select teams in this age group can be feeder teams for the local high school. These select teams may have access to the high school for practice time and school run tournaments.

In some sports tryouts may not happen, but team roster placement will. At the younger ages of 10-12, it is ideal to split teams evenly in talent if the interest is strong enough to field multiple teams within a specific organization or geographic area. Providing playing time with a variety of skill levels helps the growth of all players, physically and mentally. A single team will not dominate or get dominated in a particular game or league making it enjoyable for all.

At the age groups of 13 and 14, it is better to establish teams by skill level, such as an A team for the higher skilled and a B team for the lesser skilled. In the teenage years, players wanting to play beyond a recreational level need to learn that skill level makes a difference. Also, competition is more enjoyable when playing at your skill level.

The challenge in establishing an A team and a B team is the middle group of players. It is easy to recognize the most skilled and least skilled. The middle group of players, who could be on either team, and their parents need to be involved in discussions on team formation. It is important for each player and parent to see the good and the bad of each team's roster situation from a playing time and coaching perspective. Players at the end of the bench on the A team may be better off being a better player on the B team and vice versa. Communication between the coach and the player and the parents is really important.

SPORT SAMPLE: **For a group of 13 or 14 year old basketball players having two teams of ten players, it is easy to determine players 1-5 and 16-20 based on skill level. The middle group of ten players is where the decisions need to be made.**

If tryouts do happen, make the tryouts real. Each person trying out should have an equal chance of making the team whether they played with this team the previous season or not. No player should be placed on the team just because of past history or reputation.

At least two impartial judges with knowledge of the sport, and the head coach, should be involved in the grading of the tryouts. Other coaches can help run the tryout, but cannot be involved in the judging. Using a one through five or eight grading scale for different skill measurement is an excellent way of comparing players. And if you are grading a particular skill set, like goalkeeper in hockey or soccer, or a catcher in baseball, that is very different from the other positions on the team, be sure to measure that separately.

"Success is going from failure to failure without the loss of enthusiasm." Winston Churchill

It is better to cancel the tryout if there is no plan to change or replace players from the previous roster. A public relations tryout is a poor move by a coach when he or she knows nothing will change from the past season. A fake tryout and then keeping the same roster are poor choices for the youth involved.

Also, be careful of the players going from tryout to tryout in search of the best situation they can find. The player and the parents need to be as honest as the coach!

If a player does not make the team, a personal phone call from the coach or a meeting with the coach within a week of the tryout are the only ways to inform that player. (Also true for players making the team!) The player should know why he or she did not make the team and what skills need to be improved. A tryout should be a learning experience for the player, parents, and the coach.

"There's no harm in failing. Just pick yourself up and get back into the race. You run a little harder than the next guy and nobody will ever know you fell." A coach of Willis Reed

A parent should also be informed during that phone call or as part of that meeting. The player and parent took the time to be involved in the tryout. The coach needs to take the time in return.

SPORTS SAMPLE: **A 13-year-old soccer player was trying out for the select soccer team he had played for the previous two seasons. He was informed of not making the team by a fill in the blank form that had his name and the word "not" inserted in the blanks.**

Here are six points deducted from a coach of ages 10-14 regarding tryouts:

1. Holds fake tryouts.

2. Keeps the same roster each year.

3. Posts a public notice or holds a public meeting of who makes and does not make the team.

4. Sends out a fill in the blank form on who makes and does not make the team.

5. Does not understand specific position needs like catcher in baseball or goalkeeper in hockey or soccer requiring different mental and/or physical skills from a standard tryout in that sport.

6. Does not care about points 1-5 listed above.

Once a team has been decided on it is important for the coach to avoid the case of the whipping boy or girl. No player in this age group deserves to be mistreated physically or verbally. And no coach should use this as a motivational tool. It is not motivational for any player.

Second Inning: Ages 10-14

"Nothing will work unless you do." John Wooden

Practice time for the 10-14 year olds is the time for enjoyable discipline. Structure is the key to getting much done in little time. Here are four highlights of important practice time items from the younger age group (ages 5-9) that are critical for 10-14 year olds as well:

1. Know the players first names by the second team event and call each player by first name. All the time.

2. Have the players introduce themselves to their teammates at the first few team events.

3. Continue to teach the fundamentals of the sport.

4. Involve additional parents to help.

The coach of 10-14 year olds scores ten points for practice time if he or she does these additional items:

1. Find out from parents about any important family or school conflicts like religious events, graduations, music performances, etc. before the practice or game schedule is set up.

2. Write an outline of what you want to do for each practice and for what time period for each of the drills.

"Before everything else, getting ready is the secret of success." Henry Ford

3. Limit each drill period to 15-20 minutes.

4. Run a different drill at the same time at different workout stations for the players to go to. Be sure to split the players up so all the players are involved and no players are standing around. (With enough adult or young adult help this can be easily accomplished.)

5. Move the players from station to station for each drill.

6. Be happy with the quality of what you do and not the quantity of things you do in practice. If you plan to run five drills, but you ran three drills well and that is all you had time for, that is good!

7. Practice time should be up to two hours long for ages 10-14. Be sure to keep practice moving and keep it interesting.

8. Set up a practice schedule, with dates, at the beginning of the season and stick to it. Do not add practices unless they are voluntary. Give the players and parents the information they need to plan practices into their lives and everybody can work with it.

9. Be ready to practice at the start time. The coach needs to get there earlier if set up is involved. The player needs to get there earlier to be dressed appropriately for the respective sport.

TIME OUT: BE DRESSED APPRORPRIATELY. IF A PLAYER DOES NOT WEAR JEANS TO A BASKETBALL OR VOLLEYBALL PRACTICE, WHY DOES THE PLAYER WEAR SHORTS TO A BASEBALL PRACTICE?

10. Make sure time is included at the beginning of practice for the proper warm-ups.

11. BONUS POINT! Missing practice time in this age group is not acceptable, if the planning with parents noted above has been done. There are always good reasons for missing practice, like homework or a special family event, but a coach should not try to decide what is okay to miss for and what isn't. If a player misses any practice it should affect game playing time regardless of their reason or their skill. The importance of a planned and organized practice cannot be underestimated for a player, as well as a team.

"Discipline is not what you do to someone; it's what you do for someone." Lou Holtz

Game time is exciting in this age group, but not because the score is kept.

With the different levels of teams, you see the competitive levels come out. From recreational to school teams to select A and B teams to club and travel teams, there are a wide variety of levels of play that anyone can find their place in. Players should find the level of play that is suited to their interest and skill set. Parents should be satisfied with what their child wants. Coaches should make sure they have the time, ability, and knowledge of the sport for this age level.

"The saddest thing in competitive athletics is to see an athlete competing because he or she is required to compete, not because they desire to compete." Earl Woods

Coaches can score nine points if they make sure these game items happen for ages 10-14.

1. Reminder: Find out from parents about any important family or school conflicts like religious events, graduations, music performances, etc. before the practice or game schedule is set up.

2. Know the number of tournaments you plan to play in at the beginning of the season.

3. Prepare the league schedule as early as possible prior to the season start date.

4. Provide directions to games outside your local area.

5. Get the complete practice and game schedule to the players and parents as early as possible.

6. Get parent approval for schedule changes or additions after the season starts.

7. Inform the players and parents of when players need to arrive to be ready to play before the start time of a game and what the post game time commitment is.

8. Set expectations of playing time if there are no league rules on playing time.

9. Put all of this in writing for the players and their parents.

10. BONUS POINT! Have players play a variety of positions. It doesn't matter what the sport is, give the players a chance to experience different positions because they are still changing physically and mentally. You don't know what the player will be like in high school.

SPORT SAMPLE: **As a team of select basketball players (a feeder team for the high school) progressed through each of the age groups of 11, 12, 13, and 14, six of the 11 players on the team received all of the playing time in league games and tournaments.**

In high school, only three of the six played freshman basketball, two of the six played JV basketball and one player played for varsity in the last two years of high school.

The other players during the middle school years were not given the opportunity for playing time because of the emphasis on winning during those years. The high school paid the price in the basketball program in later years. And the players who dropped out along the way paid a higher price.

"Everybody plays. Better players play more. If you want to play more, get better." Coach Finnie

Too much emphasis is placed on winning in all sports for ages 10-14 and in all league levels, including recreational, select, club, or travel. Skill development is really the priority. Winning should be down the list. Way down the list.

Too often pictures of youth championship teams make the local newspapers in this age group. How refreshing it would be if the youth coaches would submit a team picture to the local newspaper regardless of their team record!

"I am careful not to confuse excellence with perfection. Excellence I can reach for, perfection is God's business." Michael J. Fox

There are two important reasons for deemphasizing winning in this age group:

1. Players are changing, physically and mentally. The players are at different stages of growth. While some have already started growing at age 10, others may not start their spurt until age 14. Some may even stop growing at age 12. Focusing on skill development takes into account the specific needs of any player at their current growth stage.

2. Poor coaching occurs when skill development is overlooked. If winning is emphasized, players are put in positions for a sport for the immediate gratification of a victory at the expense, in most cases, of future development of the player. Why don't coaches look at a player's parents and their physical size, and then involve the player and his parents to determine what position or positions may be best in the future, not just the present, for that player in that sport?

SPORT SAMPLE: **Youth football is a case study of emphasizing winning over skill development. The youth football coach sees the big 12-year-old player and the coach salivates. But he fails to see or does not care to see the player's petite mother and average size**

father. The big 12-year-old player is placed on the offensive line to block the other early growers on the defensive line. When this player is in high school, teammates have caught up to him physically or even passed him by. He ends up on the bench or off the high school team because he is now undersized to play on the offensive and defensive lines and does not have the skills to play in the offensive or defensive backfields. The youth football coach has let this player down for the sake of wins. And these are victories made in a youth football program.

When winning is emphasized over skill development, coaching is responsible. Here are seven points <u>deducted</u> from a coach of ages 10-14 when it comes to games:

1. Telling a player not to shoot because of skill level or coaching philosophy.

2. Pressing or running up the score when the game is out of reach.

3. Pulling a player from a game for making a mistake before there is a typical game stoppage in that sport (e.g., typical game stoppage is between innings in a baseball game or a time out/end of quarter in basketball or football).

4. Having a favorite player or players who can do no wrong.

5. Playing the same players at the same position every game.

6. Not playing players when there is no playing time requirement.

7. Receiving a technical foul or game dismissal for arguing with an official.

"Youth coaches have a responsibility to teach their players all facets of the game, including skill development, the rules, sportsmanship, and fair play." Cal Ripken

Yes, skill development, the rules, sportsmanship, and fair play are the most important items to be stressed during this age level. The players have a few years of life and sports behind them. It is easier for them to put in perspective the how and why of any sport. The players really help to deemphasize winning if handled properly.

Also, the coach is an even bigger role model at this age level since the players do have a better understanding of sports in the world. Respecting the game officials, in addition to the players and parents, provides the role model expected. Parents begin to take on the behavior of the coach for the age group of 10-14. If the coach yells at officials, some parents will follow the lead of the coach. Then the officials lose their focus on the most important reason for being there: the players!

Also, if awards are provided at season end for individual performance, the coach can make sure that multiple players get the opportunity for winning these awards or playing in all-star games. The same players being recognized for awards every year is a direct result of certain players having all the opportunities. Chances for recognition should be given to all the players.

Finally, sportsmanship and fair play are not just between teams, but also within each team. Players need to respect their teammates and treat each other properly. The coach helps to set the tone for this by the respect shown to each player and the other coaches.

"One man practicing sportsmanship is far better than a hundred teaching it." Knute Rockne

Like in the younger age group, it is up to the parents to make sure the coach is fulfilling his obligation to all players. A parent should be willing to talk in person with a coach after a practice or a game and discuss privately any concerns the parent may have. There is no need for any physical confrontation. A calm discussion between adults does help answer questions or misunderstandings. This also helps the coach eliminate the whispering in the crowd about Little Johnny and Speedy Sue.

As mentioned in the earlier age group, if a parent is unable to talk in person to the coach, the second best way is through a telephone call. These are the only choices, in person or by telephone. No e-mail, no mailed letter. If a parent has made at least two attempts to resolve their concerns with the coach and is not satisfied, then take the same steps with the organization leader. If a parent is still not satisfied, then accept the situation or find a different team or league.

Finally, ultimatums from a player or parent have no place in sport. If an ultimatum by a player or parent is given to a coach, consider it the last performance by that player on that team.

"The greatest good you can do for another is not just share your riches, but reveal to them their own." Benjamin Disraeli

Third Quarter

Warm Ups

It was the fall of freshman year in high school. Basketball tryouts were being held and the school gym was crowded with excited newcomers to high school basketball. The whistle blew. The varsity coach picked five guys to move to one side of mid-court. Five more were picked to go on the other side of the court. A jump ball was held and the five players against five players full court scrimmage began. Five minutes later the whistle blew again. Those 10 players left the court. Ten more players started a five-minute scrimmage. The scrimmaging continued for 10 new players every five minutes for the next hour.

Nobody from the "tryout" made the high school freshman basketball team.

Ages 15-18

"The imagination of a boy is healthy and the mature imagination of a man is healthy. But there is a space of life between, in which the souls is in ferment, the character undecided, the way of life uncertain, the ambition thick sighted." John Keats

This is the final four of youth sports – four years of high school athletics. Plus club and travel teams, if desired. (Or, maybe just club or travel teams if the high school competition and/or coaching are not strong enough.)

Winning takes a higher priority as a player gets to the varsity level of high school sports. Expectations in the school and in the community become greater as people want to see results in competition with other schools and communities. But fun and skill development don't have to be left at the wayside.

Before we look at the coaching levels in high school, it is important to note the differences in schools based on size and type. Size is the student enrollment for a high school and type is whether it is a public or private high school.

The size of the school makes a significant difference in the opportunity for a high school player. In a high school of two or three thousand students, there still are only 10-15 positions on the varsity basketball team or a half dozen spots on the varsity golf team. If it is a single sex school, the odds of playing a sport are even smaller.

The type of school makes a significant difference as well. Private schools typically have a recruiting capability beyond their geographic area. Changes within the public school systems allowing for open enrollment of students outside their geographic area make it easier to compete with the private school for players. But it doesn't make it any better for the average player to get an opportunity.

"Don't bother just to be better than your contemporaries or predecessors. Try to be better than yourself." William Faulkner

Some larger schools do recognize the limitations for the number of players participating in sanctioned state high school competition and offer a few sports to compete with other high schools at a less skilled level. There are also intramural sports for competition within a large high school. Or, a newer sport for high schools, like lacrosse in parts of the United States, may be started to provide a competitive outlet for more players in this age group. Finally, there are a few recreational sport leagues during the high school years, but very few. The recreational level is forgotten, unfortunately, even though almost everyone falls into the recreational level after age 18!

The challenge for smaller high schools is to be certain there are enough players trying out for the various sports. Athletic administrators at these schools need to make sure there is encouragement from all the high school coaches for multi-sport athletes.

In all sized high schools, varsity coaches of a particular sport often think their sport is the only one that is important and make the off-season program more demanding than the in-season one. Putting game limitations on off-season scheduling for a sport is one way to avoid this abuse by high school varsity coaches.

SPORT SAMPLE: **The in-season schedule for basketball in most high schools is up to a maximum of about 30 games over a 4 month winter period. The off-season schedule, using the high school name but volunteer coaches, can be twice that amount of games in spring and summer.**

Why? What about other sports? What about other activities? What about having players find their own pickup games? What about a player practicing individual skills?

It should be a wonderful time in the life of a player. The player should revel at the chance to play a sport with classmates, compete against local peers, and learn about life in the process. But the high school player also needs to realize that as he or she advances in a high school sport, the sport can no longer be just a hobby. Each year the demands increase and the player's individual commitment has to increase as well. The sport has to be a meaningful part of the player's life. The passion for the sport has to be with the player.

"If I don't put the time in, I don't deserve to play well." Juli Inkster as told to The Golf Channel

Or even, for the player, to not play at all in that sport.

Each player needs to be committed to work in the off-season to improve his or her skills. If each player is committed, there are no regrets at the end of the four years. And what a great time for players if everyone is working together.

"A team is a group of people who may not be equal in experience, talent, or education, but in commitment." Patricia Fripp

And the parents should relish this time as involved spectators. Involved by knowing what is going on in the athletic program, but also helping with fundraising opportunities and playing field work since school districts have reduced their financial support for many extracurricular activities that are of great value to high school students. What a great time for parents working together.

But only if the high school coaches help make it happen.

"We relish news of our heroes, forgetting that we are extraordinary to somebody too." Helen Hayes

Coaches play a critical role in the life of a high school athlete. How they handle tryouts, how they run practice time, and how they coach games are very important aspects of high school sports. That is just at the varsity level.

At the freshman and junior varsity levels, the high school player has to endure the training ground of coaching. Very often, the person with no or limited experience in working with young people or in the specific sport, is selected as the coach based on his or her availability, cost, or school relationship. This is too bad for the players and, even worse, for the inexperienced coach.

"Experience is the only kind of learning where the lesson follows the test." Author Unknown

Here is a three pointer on why it is too bad for the players:

1. They are taking a step back if their coaching at the previous level of recreational, select, club or travel was at a high level.

2. They may know the sport better than the high school coach from recent years of playing.

3. They may know their teammates better from playing on grade school aged teams together.

And here is a three pointer on why it is too bad for the coach:

1. He or she does not have the experience of handling player or game situations.

SPORT SAMPLE: **The players finished practice and headed off to the locker room. The coach waited in the gym for the players as they left the locker room and headed home. Except for one player, who finally came out, but was all wet. A few of his teammates threw him in the shower with his clothes on and left him soaking wet for his walk home in the middle of a Midwestern winter.**

How would a young, inexperienced coach deal with the last player out of the locker room who was ready to quit, his teammates who had done the bad deed, and all of their parents?

2. He or she will be unwilling to challenge the varsity coach on how the lower high school teams are run because of who did their hiring and their own inexperience.

3. He or she may not have their heart in it, just their school loyalty or their wallet.

The three pointers listed above are good reasons for any level of high school coaches to listen to their players for ideas on practices, games, and team functions. Most players involved in a high school sport have played much more, seen much more, and been involved much more in the sport they are playing than at any time in the history of the sport. Their input can not only give the coach some fresh ideas, but can encourage the lines of communication stay open between the coach and the team.

"I not only use all the brains that I have, but all that I can borrow." Woodrow Wilson

The toughest coaching position for high school is freshman year. Players come in from different youth programs and different schools. Usually, a large number of players come out for sports. A freshman coach then has to deal with large numbers of players who have not always played together. And still keep the varsity coach happy with how all of it is dealt with.

The junior varsity coach may have moved up the ranks from coaching freshmen in that sport or another sport. The number of team roster spots is usually less than the freshman team and you may be dealing with players who are from three different grade levels: freshman, sophomore, and junior. The varsity coach may have pushed a freshman player up or a junior player down since the junior varsity roster is usually made up of sophomores. The challenge for the junior varsity coach is working with the decisions of the varsity coach as it relates to players and a mandated style of play.

If a varsity coach moves a player up temporarily or permanently because the player has earned it with his or her ability that is okay. Okay, if the moved up player gets playing time. If a coach moves a player up because the coach wants to motivate other players on the team he or she is leaving or the team he or she is going to, that is wrong for all players involved. It never motivates other players, just discourages them. And the player moved isn't ready for the next challenge at the higher level of competition.

"When a reporter said Floyd Patterson had been downed more than most fighters," Floyd replied, "But I also got up the most." Floyd Patterson

The varsity coach usually keeps his or her eyes and ears on what is happening in his or her sport and that is both good and bad for the players. It is good if the coach really wants to develop players and has their best interest at heart. It is a problem for the players if the coach makes up his or her mind about a player at the age of 14 or 15, and doesn't account for the changes in the physical or mental ability of the player in the next few years.

Of course it is only a problem for a particular player if the varsity coach looks at the player in a negative way. If the varsity coach makes the player one of his or her "chosen ones" then the player or players become the favorites. The Chosen Ones Philosophy is a significant fault of too many varsity coaches during high school. These chosen players get the benefit of every doubt and the benefit of every good thing. The chosen players will be given multiple opportunities despite mistakes on and off the playing surface. Off-season volunteer coaches will be instructed by the varsity coach to give additional playing time to the chosen ones at the expense of other players who are also putting in the time and effort during the off-season games. This Chosen Ones Philosophy then turns off deserving players from continuing their high school athletic career for that sport. If the chosen ones don't pan out in the sport, the varsity coach has a double loss. The chosen ones are gone and deserving players have left the program. Disappointing for the players, but the varsity coach reaps what he or she sows.

SPORT SAMPLE: **In an off-season high school basketball game, the ten players were evenly divided into two groups of five by the former high school player, now the college-aged coach for basketball in the high school off-season.**

Group 1 was outscored by 10 points in the first ten minutes of the first half. Group 2 played the second ten minutes and gave the team the lead at half time.

In the second half, Group 1 was again outscored in the first ten minutes. Group 2 took over at the midway point and gave the team an eight-point lead with two minutes to go in the off-season game. Group 2 had outplayed Group 1 and had kept the team in the game.

The coach, following the obvious instruction of the varsity coach, put in a "chosen one" player from Group 1 to finish the game even though his earlier performance did not warrant it. The player from Group 2 removed from the game understood what was happening and never went to another off-season game that year.

This example can happen during any of the four years of high school. The result is the same: a lost opportunity for a player and a reduction in the number of potential players for the coach in his or her sport.

The Chosen Ones Philosophy is taken from a flawed coaches' manual. In the manual the shortsightedness of the coach is highlighted. Early judgments are made, poor decisions are implemented, and players drop from the sports program. The coach may believe the players cut themselves. No, the coach did the cutting without a true opportunity being given. The coach and the high school do not benefit. And the player suffers.

TIME OUT: THERE IS A SAYING IN PROFESSIONAL SPORTS WHEN A TEAM IS DRAFTING PLAYERS FROM COLLEGE, OR EVEN HIGH SCHOOL, TO PLAY IN THEIR SPORT, "YOU

NEVER CAN HAVE ENOUGH ESCALADES IN THE GARAGE." THAT IS ALSO TRUE DURING HIGH SCHOOL, BUT ONLY IF A VARSITY COACH LETS THE ESCALADES GET BUILT.

How a varsity coach deals with players in each of the four high school years is very important. But equally important is the style of play used by the coach. Many high school varsity coaches have minimal influence on which players attend his or her school as we discussed earlier. The poor high school varsity coach will rely on one style of play regardless of the type of players he may have in the high school program. Unlike at a college level where a coach of Florida, Marquette, or UCLA can recruit to the style of play the coach wants for that sport, a high school coach usually needs to work with what he or she gets. Unfortunately, they don't always accept this.

As stated in the Pre-Game chapter, too often high school coaches teach the same way and the same style throughout their career. Do they have 15, 20, or 25 years of experience or have they coached their first year 15, 20, or 25 times over?

"Change is the law of life, and those who look only to the past and present are certain to miss the future." John F. Kennedy

Many high school coaches learn of a style of play through a previous coach, a camp, a video, a book, or the media. They adhere to that style regardless of the player skills on their team. And they never let go of it. Even if their players' skills warrant using another style of play or even a mix of styles. Coaches need to keep learning new ways to play their sport and adapt those new ways to the skills of the players they have.

"The things you learn after you think you know it all are the most important." Claude Harmon

Good high school varsity coaches teach and use a mix of offensive and defensive styles to hit this home run.

1. They want to keep the opposition off guard.

2. They know their players, even at a high school level, have the smarts to run any type of offense or defense.

3. They know their players want to learn many styles of play because it leads to a greater challenge and to more enjoyment.

4. They want to challenge themselves each year rather than coach their first year every year.

"There are many ways of going forward, but only one way of standing still." Franklin D. Roosevelt

Another area for high school varsity coaches to reevaluate is their practice time. Longer is not necessarily better. Before school practice and, then, after school practice is not an ideal path to success either, on the playing surface or in the classroom. A planned concise practice does not have to be a marathon of three to four hours every school day. The best practices for varsity sports last no longer than two and one half hours.

Like in economics, there is a law of diminishing returns that applies to practice. The longer the practice, the less of the benefits the players keep receiving.

TIME OUT: There is no reason to practice on special holidays like Christmas Eve, Christmas Day, and Easter. None.

High school varsity coaches have great influence on young men and women beyond practice time and their style of play. How they handle game situations makes a big difference.

Unfortunately, the influence of televised sports and their announcing teams have been a detriment to the coaching of high school games. The commentary is always that players are influenced by what they see on television, but so are coaches. High school varsity coaches see the coaches pacing the sideline and being applauded by the overzealous announcers for being "into the game" or "coaching his or her heart out" or "sweating through their clothes."

TIME OUT: WHATEVER HAPPENEND TO THE JOHN WOODEN COACHING MODEL? HE SAT INTERESTED, INTENT, AND INVOLVED ON THE SIDELINE KNOWING HE HAD DONE HIS JOB IN PRACTICE TIME AND NOW IT WAS THE ROLE OF THE PLAYERS TO EXECUTE WHAT HAD BEEN PRACTICED.

Also, the reporters for televised games rarely get the coaches to admit to their failings during halftime or post game interviews. Most of the comments relate to having the players be smarter or tougher in the second half or in future competition. So it was refreshing to hear this college coach own up to his failings at halftime of a college football game.

"These kids are playing their tails off, and the coaches are screwing it up." John L. Smith

The high school varsity coaches are mirror images of many college and professional sports coaches when it comes to their local high school sports coverage. In the print coverage provided by the local press the focus is on the players' failure to perform when the outcome is not a win, but very rarely do you find a high school coach admitting to the weaknesses of their own game and/or practice strategy.

Additionally, high school varsity coaches have to be careful not to over coach. Let the players play. Let the players call the inbounds play, the check at the line of scrimmage, or the next pitch. With all the games and practices the varsity players have experienced, the players need to be given a little more credit for their length of time in the sport and in life. They know back doors, nickel defenses, and player mark ups just from watching sports and playing video games!

This is also true during the off-season game schedule. Players should be working on their individual skills, not concerned with strategy to win games or plays to be fine-tuned. Players should be excited to play and improve their skills, not burdened with over coaching by a parent or former player being directed by the varsity coach.

"Make the effort to fully achieve." John Wooden

Here is a three pointer for high school varsity coaches to score:

1. Calm down on the sidelines and let the players play.

2. Make sure a player does not get hurt trying to set an individual record.

3. Having a player score a record number of points or a team score a record number of runs against inferior competition isn't something to be proud of, especially if you have played them before.

4. BONUS POINT: Get little used players involved in games, especially in sports with penalty plays like technical foul shots, penalty kicks, and penalty shots.

SPORT SAMPLE: **In a high school varsity soccer game with Team 1 leading Team 2 by a score of 6-1 with ten minutes left to play, a penalty kick was called for Team 1. The leading scorer for Team 1, including multiple goals in this game, was the player who the foul was committed against and he was chosen by the varsity coach to take the kick against a backup goalkeeper.**

With the outcome of the game not in question, why wouldn't a varsity soccer coach choose a defender or a backup player or even the goalkeeper to have the opportunity to score a goal in a high school game on a penalty kick?

"I was a 20-20-20 man in high school basketball. I played when we were 20 points up, 20 points down, or with 20 seconds left." Bubba Paris

The final piece of high school varsity coaching is how the coach communicates with players and how he or she communicates with parents. In the Second Inning chapter we talked about how there is no need for a "whipping boy or girl" in that age group of 10-14 year olds. The same applies to high school athletes. Just because a player is older and can handle it better does not make it right.

It is important for the coach to treat the players like they would students in the classroom. The court, the field, the pool, is the classroom for players and coaches. These young men and women need and deserve the same respect as athletes as they get as students.

If the varsity coach makes a change in the starting lineup or the varsity roster during the season, it needs to be communicated individually to the players affected. The players have worked throughout the season, and hopefully the off-season, and deserve to know why a change is being made and what they need to do to improve. And the communication needs to continue with each player for the rest of the season. They need to be encouraged to keep working at their game. No player should be abandoned for athletic reasons in any sport.

Like in the ages 10-14, there is no place for ultimatums by players or parents on playing time or positions in high school age sports. If an ultimatum is given, it should be the last performance by the player on that team.

Finally, the coach needs to stay positive with his or her players. High school varsity coaches need to remember how they would want to be treated if they were still playing.

"But if I coached you, and if I was always telling you all about the things you were doing wrong, you wouldn't play good for me. You'd be all nervous and tight. When I tell my guys I love them, I mean it, I know they're out there

playing their best for me, and that they love me just as much as I love them. There is no reason for me not to stay positive." Coach Tony Ingle as told to ESPN.com

Since the playing surface is the classroom for the sport and the time spent by players in the sport during the season is usually greater than the time spent on Math or English or Science or Physical Education in classroom hours during that season, it is time for varsity coaches to start parent/player/coach conferences during each of the high school grade levels. The educational curriculum mandates it. The athletic program should as well.

It is time for high school coaches to provide a report card to player and parents during the season and discuss how things are being done, what progress athletically is being made, and what improvements are in order. Coaches don't have to fear this anymore than they have any trepidation over standard parent/teacher conferences in Math, English, Science, or Physical Education. Interested players and parents would show up at the conference the same way that the interested student and parents show up for the academic conference. The communication line would be open. And the whispering in the stands would be reduced.

"People don't change when you tell them they should. They change when they tell themselves they must." Thomas Friedman from his book, The World Is Flat

Fourth Round

Warm Ups

The 13-year-old select team was in the middle of their baseball season. Before a game, a mother of one of the players, a player who had missed part of the first half of the season with an illness, wanted to make sure her son would be getting more playing time. She said he would be the only one of the 13 players on the team to play high school baseball so he should be getting as much playing time as possible.

Five years later and he never played any high school baseball. Ten of his teammates played high school baseball and four of the 10 started for their varsity teams for at least two years.

All Ages

After the "Massacre at Winged Foot" in 1974, Sandy Tatum, then chairman of the United States Golf Association championship committee was asked why the organization was trying to embarrass the best golfers in the world at the difficult Winged Foot course.

"We're not trying to embarrass them," Tatum replied. "We're trying to identify them." from Golf Digest

The same is true with this book. Identify what needs to be done by a coach in any sport from ages 5-18. The purpose, stated earlier, is to make the sports life better for all of those involved by opening up the lines of communication between the three key groups in youth sports: players, parents, and coaches!

In the last half-century of sports, many things have changed. Equipment has improved. Uniforms are better. Athletic training is more scientific. Sports information is more accessible. Media coverage is more available. There are more teams in more sports. And more players involved in sports than ever before.

But one important item in sports has not changed. The coaching in sports for the ages of 5-18 is stuck in a time warp. The weaknesses in coaching prevalent 30 and 40 years ago are still around today. Those weaknesses can be summarized into the four majors for each age grouping:

Ages 5-9

1. Not giving every player a chance.
2. Players standing around at practice.
3. Not focusing on fundamentals.
4. Not keeping parents informed.

Ages 10-14

1. Limiting a player to one position.
2. Holding a poor tryout.
3. Emphasizing winning.
4. Not keeping players and parents informed.

Ages 15-18

1. Inexperienced and untrained coaches.
2. Coaching only one way.

3. Chosen Ones Philosophy.
4. Not keeping players informed and involved.

If you are a player today, you probably wish for more appreciation, more opportunity, and more responsibility.

If you are a parent today, you probably shake your head at the lack of progress in the coaching of players in all sports. Progress in accepting all of the changes noted above that make players better physically, and smarter mentally, in the sports they play.

If you are a coach today, you should realize now that life long learning goes with the position. Coaches need to stay abreast of what is happening in society and in their sport. And see how those changes impact the way they coach and how they communicate. And that communication is the way to win. Not win games. But win over the players and the parents - the people you are coaching for every day throughout the season.

"If you think education is expensive, try ignorance."
Derek Bok

More importantly, the number of possible ways to communicate between players, parents, and coaches has increased over the years. Through cell phones, email and websites, coaches can reach out to the players and parents easily. But little progress in communication has occurred even when the best way to communicate between player or parent and coach hasn't changed at all. Face to face communication is the best way now, like it could have been, like it should have been, during the last fifty years.

"You have to accept that what seems important to you may not be very important to other people." Hubert Humphrey

But it cannot be accepted any longer. Better coaching is important because sports can be an exciting part of a player's life during their youth and can be extended throughout adulthood. Players can learn so much about life from the games they play. It is not the wins and losses, the trophies and all-star teams, or the unending practices and endless off-season. But it is what they learned about themselves, how to work with other people, and the memories they take away. The youth of today and tomorrow deserve better. Players should be turned on, not turned off by coaches. Players should have wonderful thoughts about the people who lead them on the playing surface, not deep regret for having participated or never given a chance to participate.

Sports also can be an important part of parenting because of the numerous life experiences gathered from teamwork to parent/player talk time to meeting other parents. Parents should relish the chance for others to help their sons and daughters learn about life, not shudder at what opportunities are being wasted for their children by coaches who don't know or haven't kept up with their sport, or don't know how or don't want to communicate to players and parents.

Most youth through high school coaches want to make a difference in a player's life. The commitment of their time and effort is impressive. But leave the inflated egos behind. Let's have the difference made be a positive one for the player and for the parents.

As stated in the Pre-Game chapter, many coaches use the phrase "I'm in it for the kids" when talking of issues with the players, parents, officials, or the games. If it is for the kids, then let's not be concerned with just the wins, the trophies, the all-star teams, the college scholarship dreams, and the professional contract myths.

Let's make sure the kids have a great experience playing the sport, working with teammates, and being communicated to in a responsible way. And any parent can be happy with that result.

A coach can make a positive difference. These are the reasons coach is the best five letter word you can be called.

"Man may penetrate the outer reaches of the universe. He may solve the very secret of eternity itself. But for me, the ultimate experience is to witness the flawless execution of the hit-and-run." Branch Rickey

Post-Game

Like after any sporting event, handshakes or hugs go out to:

my wife, Cherie, for accepting my time away coaching and playing.

my children, Brian and Tim, for accepting me as a father, coach, and player.

my parents, who taught me to play and to be there when my children played organized sports.

the players I coached or played with.

the parents of the players I coached.

the other coaches who helped me with developing players and people.

the game officials who helped in player and people development.

my editor, Carolyn Finnie, for making the final product better.

my reviewers: Cherie, AJ VanHandel and Larry Hogan for sharing their insights.

you, the reader, for making the world of sports a better place to play in.

"If you played the game the right way, played the game for the team, good things would happen" Ryne Sandberg

www.ingramcontent.com/pod-product-compliance
Ingram Content Group UK Ltd.
Pitfield, Milton Keynes, MK11 3LW, UK
UKHW041839200726
13854UKWH00003BA/1223